Writer's Guilt

AKHILA KRISHNA

BookLeaf Publishing

India | USA | UK

Presentation by *BookLeaf Publishing*

Web: www.bookleafpub.com

E-mail: info@bookleafpub.com

ISBN: 9789360944889

First edition 2024

"To John Joy, my forever home, where his love uplifts me on my bluest days, his eyes reflect the good in my heart in the warmest glow, a love I behold from the rear window of my heart."

ACKNOWLEDGEMENT

The journey of bringing my first book to life has been a dream come true, and it's all thanks to the amazing people who've been with me every step of the way! First and foremost, my incredible husband John Joy - your support and belief in me have meant the world. From our early days of friendship to now, you've been my biggest cheerleader, and I'm so grateful for your constant encouragement.

Huge thanks also to my wonderful family for their unwavering support and guidance. Your love and faith in me have been a constant source of strength, and I feel so lucky to have you all in my life.

And last but definitely not least, a massive thank you to my fabulous friends Athulya and Amy - you guys have been my sounding board, my confidantes, and my biggest fans. Your belief in me has given me the courage to chase my dreams, and I'm forever grateful for your friendship.

To each and every one of you, thank you from the bottom of my heart for helping me turn my

dream into a reality. I couldn't have done it
without you!"

PREFACE

In the pursuit of creating *Writer's Guilt*, my debut poetry collection, the complexities of trauma, healing, and self-discovery are explored. Through the poems, the darkest corners of human experience are delved into, seeking to illuminate the path towards resilience and transformation.

As Richard Powers so aptly puts it, "Life assembles itself on accumulating mistakes." This quote resonates deeply with the themes of the poetry, which grapple with the idea that mistakes and struggles are not failures, but rather the building blocks of growth and redemption.

Through vulnerability and shared experiences, the poems aim to inspire readers to embrace their own journey, find solace in the darkness, and emerge stronger, wiser, and more radiant than ever. I hope these poems will resonate with you and provide a sense of understanding and solidarity, reminding you that even amid chaos, beauty and hope can be found.

Sunset

The one you despised, you are him now.
In your glory, I bled gold.

Convince my heart, was I ever enough?
Fire and fumes, stay hidden love.

Don't stray, you won't find much.
Innocence was long dead.

Courtyard mirror and the bloody nose,
Witness a real storm.

Broken bones and burned skin;
Mind palace stained in blood.

Puppet Show

Pregnant dots of match-fixing,
Pulling me down like gravity.

Standing on top of an open wound,
Smiling upon my childhood.

Yearning for them to save me once,
But their lips sewed twice in guilt.

Ticks the clock, and another bruise to heal;
A menace that keeps me awake all night.

Welled-up eyes soon dried out and bloodshot;
Sandworms crawling out of my sore throat.

Trapped inside a game of snakes and ladders,
Drunk on my pain, a puppet master.

Rear Window

Black is his colour, his salvation, his knight.
Vanilla was the sky, when I kissed him so tight.
A quick bite to his lips; it bleeds of caramel
light.
Oh my Solomon, take me to the promised land
Where the Vineyard blooms in moonlight.

Open my eyes and signal them the daffodils
Of our love, a union so godly and pure.
Let them cry and bend me onto your arms
With frolics of Thor's thunder and Zeus's
Lighting accompanied.

The Rain came pouring through the open rear
Window later that night.
Sweeping off my feet, I flew, my body and soul
Rose bright.
Only to Drown in the silver pool of evermore
With our hands intertwined.

Destiny

Honey child, an antelope of cosmic space,
Floating high on a lover's hot cup of coffee.
Rainbow-skinned god, watching over us all,
Caress colours of a love story on budding skies.
Summer air, this love is an artistic flair,
Safe, between the magic of his wise arms.

Home Ground

Trees show off their honest skeleton forms,
Fallen leaves whispering secrets as the wind
Blows
Clementine whiskey skies adorned my country
Meadows,
Silver kettle whistles sweet melodies of home.

Echoes

Forever lost in the eye of the tornado,
Unrequited at the rosy corridors of youth.
Listening to the violin blues of rain,
An unending concert of serene sad songs.
Icy crystal tears bless breathing contours,
Bidding farewell to curvy plateau of deserted
Dreams.

Misery

Unsettled like dead bugs on stagnant mucky
water,
inside a valentine glass vase of withered
wildflowers.
Dancing to a forgotten love song under a disco
ball,
unfolding my neatly layered origami flowers of
grief.

Guilt

Tied to a cross of consequences,
An advocate of guilt.

Churned through my brain and found
Tokens of lies draped in Satin.

Guilty as the ring on my finger
A false promise of forever.

Devine intervention, for a ninny
Time is a villain.

Apology

A long time ago, cruel little kids drowned me in
a river of insecurities.
My heavy brown body made me a favourite prey
for their muse hunting.
I tried to fight back, but I sank gracefully,
touching the sleeping riverbed.
Later, dismembered parts of me washed up on
the shore breathing,
but some things were too heavy and got lost in
the river shallows.

I saw what was left of me reflected in the river's
uneasy waters.
I only had pure hate for what I saw and wanted
to escape this living tragedy.
Took the pebbles around me and scratched hard
on my skin to lighten it,
seeking all the praise that followed with it which
was what I thought I deserved.

I starved and starved until my thighs didn't look
heavy like they said.
my flabby arms they love to point at became thin
like matchsticks.
I tried to scrape pieces off me to fit into the
infamous silicone mould.

they called it, "desirable." Desperate, I burned
and ran towards a pretty size.

But what I lost in that riverbed never came to
light, even with my pretty size in hand.
Now, I'm lost, trapped in an empty shell, and my
regrets are my only company.
I am guilty of shoving mean insecurities down
my innocent young self's throat.
My apologies, dear girl who drowned in my
cowardice, for not loving you unconditionally.

Last Happy Hour

Coffee, cigarettes and ten thousand blueprints
later,
I am still here, at the last happy hour I left us.
Our world is old-fashioned, and conversations in
secret dialects,
I am still here, at the last happy hour I left us.
Your laugh slaps witty remarks, and a never
setting sun for eyes.
I am still here, at the last happy hour I left us.
You were driving but I had the map to a perfect
angle for a shot.
A wild ride to tame the most hunted and desired
beast, womanhood.
Sands through the hourglass, marking the frantic
end of an era.
I am still here, at the last happy hour I left us.
We rolled and aced one last bone and locked up
a place once we called home.
My heart broke, lungs collapsed in the silent
goodbyes of the quiet journey back.
Till the next time, but we both Lied.
And I am still here, stuck at the last happy hour
where we became strangers.

Fragile Love

Made a grand baroque castle of romance on
Quicksand.
Plastic flowers at a forgotten grave with a
crumbling tombstone.
A tale to hold onto, cherish, and breathe life into
until the next stop.

Pin Drop

Eerie silence of ego battles crushing in,
Suffocating in the heights of a heavy sin.
Joking in lores of angst a circus treat
Desperate humour for a drowning heartbeat.

Runny eyes from the burnout of a blind passion.
Four walls fighting to contain the scary voices in
action.
Episodes of turmoil dethroning an instilled
crown
In a locked away safe, a fragile wedding gown.

Matches soaked in blood inviting divine
darkness,
Painting a guiding star in the night's cold
canvas.
Familiar tender voices fading along with rattled
hope
A ship made of gold sailing away without scope.

Secret

A secret beneath my cotton-stuffed bed coat.
Hidden under a precious gift with love.

I wash my filth off, several times a day.
Still, my skin itches with sin all day

A twinge awaits my heart, a shattering
devastation.
For soon one day you will catch me, red in the
act.

Stockholm

A haunting call that lasted for years,
Interrupting my whispers of prayers.
In the confinement of an evil eye,
One hundred eighty-two weeks in pitch black.
Harnessing inner power and building up my
might,
To break the fourth wall into my freedom's light.
One windy morning, my silence finally broke.
The station went quiet as my truth spoke.
I took a flight with my regained wings,
To embrace my long-lost freedom.
My voice is heard and now I am truly free.

Apocalypse

Pain-inflected sour patches amidst a silent war
A lot to unpack, so let's start at the very
beginning of the clock.
Fingers pointed, blames exchanged and a
heaven-lost in the haze.
Insight blossomed, but jealousy burned down the
Babel's gaze.

Obsolete idols worn out by the wheel of time.
Empty pews and altars with no one left to serve.
A few thousand apostasies later, True horror
lurks in plain sight.
One vast universe to explore, yet a fear of the
unknown holds tight.

Escapism

Making exits, cooping in with ache I lay,
Tiptoeing through my confused mind all-day
Missing a beating Heart, I need to reclaim
Luxuriating in pain, my fragile frame

Wearing delicate glass skin, hauntingly bright
Invisible hands follow me to sleep at night
Reaching out for warmth into the void
My great escape into hallucinated joy.

Muted

Unassailable snowy marble walls of silence
slowly rise
Outfitted in warm fresh ink stains of stark truth
that never dies
Benighted dusty letters sent to collapsing crypts
unfold
Secrets of the butchered history of Red Queens,
a tale so old.

In chambers of old chronicles, sharp lies ring
throughout
Tied in shackles of misogyny, a mournful
whimpering sight.
No scribbled pages left whispering their truth or
name
Lost in the womb of existence, their rightful
fame.

Now these marble walls slowly disintegrate and
wear out
Holding back cherished memories of unsung
heroine's plot.
Legacy of Red Queens, a tale of sacrifice and
pain
A story no one will ever hear, echoing in bane.

Devotion

Angels revealing their winged monstrosities,
Fear and devotion are now a toxic blend,
Holy, holy, holy, a desperate cry.
A venomous serpent latching to seize control,
Rims of its scales, a grieving night grey.

Holy, holy, holy, all day every day,
Ramblings through the darkness on repeat.

Alleged Lore

Shadow of my past, a demon at hunting.
Big yellow eyes, a leash around my neck.
The pieces fell where they did,
And he played the game the best.
His toxic grip had me choking.
A teenage dream altered,
Now a breathing fever dream.
A captive to his tantrums,
A coward under a knitted blanket fortress

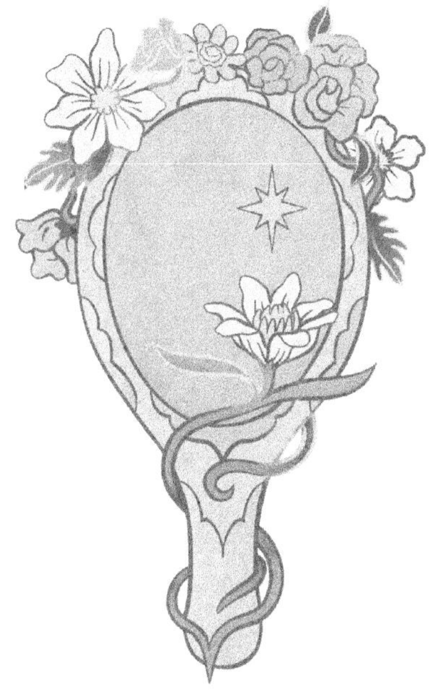

Potions

Secrets are carefully crafted poisons,
Made with bitter-sweet, fatal mock-tails of lies.
Modulus operandi for twisted minds,
Wearing woollen cloaks of starless skies.

Trickster

Pouring rain and swollen rivers,
Moonlit water beneath my feet.

Found a kingdom from a flecked picture book,
Came in a petulant shadow in a cupcake gown.

My anxiety, a trickster to play their charm,
Swirling and entrapped in a vicious cycle.

Breathing my way out of their power,

Popping some pills to make me a new slate.

Bluff Master

The seven deadly sins crossed off my hot pink
checklist,
All my misdeeds lead my name to fate's deadly
blacklist.
Sitting on top of my victims, holding onto my
proud thunder,
My blood now tastes of power, an addiction for
my existence.
I caught his omniscient hunter eyes in a glorious
fumble,
Fate arrived tailored in a bejewelled blinding
suit of justice,
To reckon my beloved old twin towers of
wrongdoings.
My name was inscribed atop his scroll in bloody
ink.
With transgressions catalogued, to drag me off
my flesh throne,
But I, a cunning warrior, one faceless god of
deceits,
Serve him a platter of slow-cooked, spicy lies
He savoured each bite, his pupils dilated with
delight,
Until, with a polite farewell, he departed, his
plate pristine.

Tenant

One clandestine deal, for a white-collar devil's
act
Living rent-free in my head, a holdover tenant's
pact
He breathes through my cells, infesting in my
mind
Invading my childhood being sinister and
unkind.

Under the bridge, my deep secrets are buried,
Between your knees, my innocence sealed.
Fondlings of torment cried out helpless pleas
A lost childhood, broken doll, a predator's tease.

Slicing me up to the beat of your ominous jazz
sound
Easily swaying, my soul forever unbound.
Stained from a nightmare, a joy forever sold.
Skin shedding away showcasing rotten flesh's
mold.

Guiding Jack

Gliding across the frozen, enchanted river,
Guiding me out of the misty, howling forest of
grim legends.
An Arctic Jack hare in a ruby velvet suit,
Wearing a pair of charming, honey-glazed eyes
to get lost in.
His tantalising trail, a sweet note of perfume,
Extracted from blushing, fresh strawberry
cheeks.

Writer

I am dressing up my pages one by one,
With Persian blue shades of a sad mind.

Ink prints and spots covering my palm lines.
My rambling thoughts, most of it such raff.

Except these parchments carry a heavy heart.
Saving my soul away from ghosts of a past life.